GW00992848

British Commonwealth Edition
Published by Scripture Union
London, England.

North American Edition Including Canada
Published by Regal Books
A Division of G/L Publications
Ventura, California, USA

© Gordon Stowell 1985

First Edition 1985   Reprinted 1988

Co-edition arranged with the help of
Angus Hudson, London

Printed and Bound in Great Britain by
Purnell Book Production Ltd., Paulton, Bristol

Little Fish Books about Bible Animals

The Camel's Journey

illustrated by Gordon Stowell

My master is a very wise man. He
lives in a beautiful palace in the east.
My job is to take him to distant
places to meet other wise men.

My master studies the stars. One day
a new star appeared in the sky. He
was very excited about it.

He looked in his big books and
spoke to other wise men about it.

My master knew the appearance of
this star meant that a new King had
been born.

We were to go on a long journey.
Enough food was packed to last a
long time.

'We started to follow the bright star.
Other wise men came along with us.

We travelled by night and by day.
We went over mountains and
through valleys.

Robbers chased us more than once. I became very weary, but still the star led us on.

At last we arrived in Jerusalem. The
wise men told King Herod about
their journey.

He was angry to hear that a new King
had been born. He sent us on to
Bethlehem.

We were nearly at the end of our
journey at last. The star led us
onward until it stopped over the
little town called Bethlehem. Was
this the end of our travels?

Down the hill we went and came to a
house. The wise men got off. They
unwrapped the special gifts they had
brought all the way with them.

The door was opened. The wise men went in. Peeping round the edge of the doorway I could see them kneeling down in front of a mother with her child.

The presents were gold,
frankincense and myrrh, and the
child was called Jesus.

**Read about the Christmas story in Matthew
chapter 2 and Luke chapter 2.**

Two by Two

Billy Goat escapes!

The Christmas Donkey

The Camel's Journey

 Little Fish Books

The Storks and the King

Fed by Ravens

The Lost Sheep is found

Little Donkey's Big Day

about Bible Animals